If You Only Knew My Story

Bertha J. Banks

Copyright © 2023 Bertha J. Banks.

All rights reserved. No part of this book may be reproduced, stored, or transmitted by any means—whether auditory, graphic, mechanical, or electronic—without written permission of both publisher and author, except in the case of brief excerpts used in critical articles and reviews. Unauthorized reproduction of any part of this work is illegal and is punishable by law.

ISBN: 979-8-88640-845-4 (sc)
ISBN: 979-8-88640-846-1 (hc)
ISBN: 979-8-88640-847-8 (e)

Because of the dynamic nature of the Internet, any web addresses or links contained in this book may have changed since publication and may no longer be valid. The views expressed in this work are solely those of the author and do not necessarily reflect the views of the publisher, and the publisher hereby disclaims any responsibility for them.

One Galleria Blvd., Suite 1900, Metairie, LA 70001
1-888-421-2397

Table of Contents

Introduction vii
Chapter 1:   Clothing Made by Mom 1
Chapter 2:   Free from the Cotton Farm 3
Chapter 3:   Bad Dreams as a Child 5
Chapter 4:   Growing Up as a Child 7
Chapter 5:   Learning about Sex 9
Chapter 6:   My First Real Job as a Teenager 11
Chapter 7:   Abusive Relationships 13
Chapter 8:   Trying It Again 15
Chapter 9:   Prayer 17
Chapter 10: Moved to Columbus 19
Chapter 11: Near-Death Experience of Childbirth 20
Chapter 12: Ended the Marriage 22
Chapter 13: Life-Changing Experience 24
Chapter 14: Raising Three Children 25
Chapter 15: Before Coming Back to the Lord Jesus Christ 27
Chapter 16: Never Say Never on What You Are Going to Do 30
Chapter 17: Testimony No. 1 34
Chapter 18: Testimony No. 2 36
Chapter 19: Dreaming of Marriage 39

Chapter 20:	Running from the Calling	40
Chapter 21:	Hurt Beyond Measure	42
Chapter 22:	Church Deception	46
Chapter 23:	Separation in the Home	48
Chapter 24:	Loss of Church Memberships	50
Chapter 25:	Spent Time from Home	52
Chapter 26:	Awake—Accident in Dream before It Happened	55
Chapter 27:	Move Out of the Problems	58
Chapter 28:	Only God Can Put Pieces Back Together	62
Chapter 29:	Going through Divorce Causes Pain	64
Chapter 30:	Divorce Leaves Grief	66
Chapter 31:	Can We Be Bound Up and Not Know It?	68
Chapter 32:	Jesus Will Put Our Life in Perspective	70
Chapter 33:	New Beginning	75
Chapter 34:	My Achievement	81
Chapter 35:	Letting Go	84
Chapter 36:	Learning about Abuse and Domestic Violence	86
Chapter 37:	Abused	88
Chapter 38:	Recognizing Child Abuse and What Parents Need to Know	90
Chapter 39:	Domestic Violence	93
Chapter 40:	Prayer	95
Chapter 41:	In with the New and Let Go of What's Behind	97
Notes		99

I dedicate this book to Pastor Daisy Milner my adopted mother, who has great wisdom. To my son Avery C. Smith and my daughter's Michelle Rash, Cynthia A. Land and Ravon Smith. To my grandchildren and great grand-children.

Introduction

The reason why I chose this cover page for my book was because of the barbed-wire fence where a little girl stood up on it. It was because my sister told me a true story about how she would go down by the hogs pen every day, climbed up on the barbed-wire fence, stood up on the second row on the fence, and looked up to heaven and prayed for God to send us some food to eat. When my sister was talking to me, I saw a vision of what she was saying and praying to God for a miracle to take place. I saw in a vision as if it was me praying to God for the same thing to come to pass. That vision and what I saw has never left me. It is with me until this day, the true story of the prayer. My sister's prayer took place where we lived on the plantation for years as sharecroppers. Thank God for change.

I'll let you know about my life as a child and the type of lifestyle I lived and the abuse and bullying growing up, the hurt and pain, sickness, and near-death experience I went through. I'll share how I survived and how I raised my three children and worked hard to make a life for them to complete high school and to further their education and to be successful men and women. I'll also talk about the abusive husbands and infidelity in my marriages and the likes of trust, hurt, abuse, and suffering in my life.

I was born in Santuc, South Carolina, to Willie Land Sr. and Rosa Jeter Land with a family of thirteen siblings, and I am the thirteenth sibling. When I was a child growing up, I had hopes for the present and future that one day I would grow up to be a Palm Beach based beauty, go to Hollywood, and marry a movie star. That was my dream when I was growing up as a child.

My father was a sharecropper; he was an overseer over the cotton farm. My mother was a nanny working away from the home and coming home on the weekends. I was brought up on the cotton plantation and raised up in church. We had to walk three and a half miles to church every Sunday. We stayed all day at church and came home after the last service at night. Church members brought food to share with everyone in church; that was the way church members did things in the South back in the day. Today we do good if we can get the church body to stay for two hours.

At the age of five, I was picking, planting, and hoeing cotton among other chores around the farm. My siblings and I had to stay out of school for weeks at a time to work in the cotton farms. In spring, we had to plant cotton. In summer, we had to hoe cotton, and in the fall of that year, we had to harvest cotton. At the end of the harvest year, we only received a pair of shoes or coat, maybe a dress. We were farmer kids. Our parents grew all our food on the farm except for few selected items which our parents would purchase at the store. We were healthy and strong. We were not able to go to the doctors; we used home health care, which was home remedies. We did not have any money or health insurance, so we could not afford to go to the doctors.

Chapter 1

Clothing Made by Mom

Farmer families and their kids are very poor. We as a family did not have much, but we had each other, and we loved each other. My mother made most of our clothes. Some of my dresses were made out of clover sack bags, which was a cotton sack. After all the flour was used out of the clover sack bag, Mother took the flour sack, cut the bag open, washed it, and made our dresses for my sisters and me; the flour sack came in twenty-five-pound bags. My mother would take the sack, cut it apart, place it on the pattern, cut it out, and made our dresses. I am not ashamed to let you know where I came from and how I survived. Everyone in school knew we had on clover- sack dresses. Oh, we were not the only kids who were wearing flour sack bags (clover) for dresses. Wearing the clover-sack dresses—that chapter was closed in our lives when my mother got a job working as a nanny—no more flour-sack dresses.

I am so glad that bullying was not an issue then as it is today. It was bad enough. The kids would make fun of our clover-sack dresses. I had to stand up for myself because one day I was being bullied, and my brother made me stand up to the bully for myself to keep me from being bullied by the kids again at school. And coming home from school, kids would pick on me on the bus, and walking home I stopped the bully and stood up to the bully. Today when kids get bullied, they go back to school with a gun and kill the kid that bullied them; sometimes when kids are being bullied, they kill themselves. They cannot take the pressure. They act as if it is the only way out. Stand up to the bully. Talk to someone about the problem; do not think there is no way out.

When I was twelve years old, I was baptized. I did not know what I was doing at that age, but I did know it was the right thing to do. I looked forward to going to church every Sunday. There was Mrs. Jane who had two kids with her every Sunday. Her kids wore beautiful dresses with three layers of wide petticoat slip under their dresses. Mrs. Jane did not want us to touch their dresses; she said we would get it dirty. Mrs. Jane turned her nose up in the air and looked at us and took her two daughters and walked into the church. That was a bad feeling of rejection. I grew up in church until I was fifteen years old, and I stopped going to church. I started working picking peaches in the summer at Sunny Slope Farm Peach Orchard Incorporated so I could buy my clothing for the school season. The cotton-picking days were over. Thanks be to God.

> "I have strength for all things in Christ who empowers me [I am ready for anything and equal to anything through him who infuses inner strength into me; I am self-sufficient in Christ's sufficiency]" (Phil. 4:13 AMPC).

Chapter 2

Free from the Cotton Farm

I was so glad when my mother said to us, the last three children at home, that we did not have to pick cotton on the cotton farm any longer. My mother had saved up enough money working as a nanny to build a house for her family. My mother worked as a nanny and came home every Friday evening, went back to work on Sunday evening to work as a nanny all week away from her family. My mother had a room at her employer's home where she stayed all week, worked, and made $12.50 per week. My mother worked as a nanny for sixteen years. I thank God for my mother because she saved up enough money for sixteen years to have a house built for her family so the family could have a place where we could call our own home. My father and my brothers built the house, and my mother became a homeowner. That was a great day. We were no longer bound by a man on the cotton farms and plantation law. Praise God.

> "Can anything ever separate us from Christ's love? Does it mean he no longer loves us if we have trouble or calamity, or are persecuted, or hungry, or destitute, or in danger, or threatened with death? No, despite all these things, overwhelming victory is ours through Christ, who loved us" (Rom. 8:35, 37 NLT).

When I was a little girl, I did not understand why my mother would go away and leave us, my sisters and brothers, all week long at home with our father. I do know now more than ever that she was making and leaving a legacy for her children in the best way she knew how. I cry sometimes when I think about my mother and all the sacrifices, all the name-calling and abuse she went through for her family while working. My mother said that her employer and family would leave money lying around on the tables and other places in the home to see if she would steal the money. My mother said that she would dust around it and leave it there on the tables and sweep around it with the vacuum and leave it on the floors where she saw it. Employers would do that all the time to see if we as black people would steal.

> "And that's not all. You will have complete and free access to God's kingdom, keys to open any every door: no more barriers between heaven and earth, earth and heaven. A yes on earth is a yes in heaven, a no on earth is a no in heaven" (Matt. 16:19 NIV).

Chapter 3

Bad Dreams as a Child

When I was a little girl, I had bad dreams until I was twelve years old. I could see things; some of them were evil spirits. I had bad dreams every night as soon as I closed my eyes. In my bed I could look down through the mattress, and the only thing I could see were red coals of fire and fire just burning as far as I could see down. I was at a point wherein I was afraid to go to sleep. I would wake up out of my sleep screaming and howling at the top of my lungs. My father would come into my bedroom and get me and put me in the bed with him. How many know that there was no child abuse from my father? He was just a father protecting, loving, and watching over his child.

I felt safe with my father, and I went back to sleep. After I got into my teen years, the bad dreams stopped. I was always a dreamer and still do dream. I had so many dreams. I'd written most of them down. Some of them had come to pass, and some had not. Some of my dreams were warnings to other family members or other people in reality. They were able to escape or turn that dream around in their lives. The pain, hurt, suffering, and near-death experience that was in the dream turned around for the good, and the bad things did not happen.

> "And afterward I will pour out My Spirit upon all flesh; and your sons and daughters shall prophesy, your old men shall dream dreams, your young men shall see visions" (Joel 2:28 AMPC).

Chapter 4

Growing Up as a Child

When I was a child, I grew up with my three brothers. I had two sisters that were a little older than I am. My oldest brothers and sisters were old enough to be my parents, and my parents were old enough to be my grandparents. When I became a teenager, my oldest sibling was a grown-up and moved away from home. I am the thirteenth child, which means the baby of the family. I was spoiled by most of my siblings.

I grew up with my young brothers; I was called a tomboy. I only had brothers to play with. They taught me how to be tough. I could do most of the things they could do around the home.

We lived so far in the woods in a house in the country where there was no other house nearby. I did not know about sex than only playing cowboys and Indians with my brothers. We made stick for guns to play with since our parents could not afford the plastic guns.

Do you understand where I am coming from? Kids do not understand how we played with nothing and made something out of it and had fun with what we had. Kids today do not have enough patience to make do with what they have. I knew the day would come when God will supply all our needs according to his riches in glory.

> "But my God shall supply all your need according to his riches and glory by Christ Jesus" (Phil. 4:19 KJV).

Chapter 5

Learning about Sex

I did not know about sex back in those days. Our parents did not tell us about sex back then. If you asked them about sex, they would say that we were being fast or hot. Hot was the name that parents would give their children if they thought they were fast, or they would say, "Smelling yourself." Those were the things parents would say to their children if we asked them questions and about sex. Parents would have all kinds of answer to avoid the issue or question than telling us the truth about sex in the olden days.

Are we glad that parents are not that way today? Modern-day parents are different in teaching and educating their kids with information. That was the way parents were raised and taught. Parents did not educate their children on sex then, but they do now. Parents would not talk to their children about sex. I did not know about sex or what a monthly cycle (period) was until I was twelve years old. In my class, there were two older teenage girls who were two years older than we were who shared with us what a monthly cycle (period) was and explained it to us. So when I started my monthly cycle, I knew what to expect. Parents and teachers would not educate their children and students on things such as sex and the like.

And now schools are letting the teacher pass out condoms to help teens to just say yes to having sex. Would you educate your teens by giving them condoms? Schools are not telling teens what the consequences are and what it would cost them in their future.

> "Train up a child in the ways he are she should go, and when they get old they will not depart from it" (Prov. 22:6 AMP).

If I had known some things about sex and boys at an early age, I would not have gotten pregnant and had a baby after high school. I had my two daughters before marriage. I thank God for my two daughters. They are strong, independent women with good education and good jobs. I love them. There is nothing I would not do for my daughters. I can say they are a blessing. Both my daughters have worked hard to have a career that is so promising and needed. My parents could not afford to send their children to college, my twelve siblings and me. But later on in 1985, I went to learn word processing at a secretarial school and received my diploma.

> I run from sexual sin! No other sin clearly affects the body as this one does. For sexual immorality is a sin against your body. Don't you realize that your body is the temple of the Holy Spirit, who lives in you and was given to you by God? You do not belong to yourself, for God bought you with a high price. So you must honor God with your body. (1 Cor. 6:18–20 NLT)

Chapter 6

My First Real Job as a Teenager

Oh, by the way, when I was fifteen years old, I had to work at my mother's job as a nanny for one summer. Before I got the job at Kentucky Fried Chicken, I worked as a nanny for the summer. On one Friday night, my mother's employer was bringing me home. He started making sexual passes at me, and he took me down in the wooded areas instead of taking me home. I jumped out of the car and ran as fast as I could through the woods, and he could not find me. When I knew he was going, I got back on the road and started walking home. When I got home, I did not tell my mother about what had happened. On Sunday evening, it was time for me to go back to work. I said to my mother I was not ever going back over there to work again. Mother did not pressure me about going back. I do believe that my mother knew why I was not going back to work. My mother was a wise woman.

That was when I applied and got my first job in the city at Colonel Sanders's Kentucky Fried Chicken. It was my first real job at the age of sixteen. I knew I had moved on up in lifestyle. I felt free and no longer bound to my past lifestyle and the cotton fields. After high school, I stayed with my parents for a while, and then I moved in with my sister in the city. I started working at the cotton mill for three years and rented my first apartment in the city. I can remember my apartment number today, 227. I can never forget that apartment; it was the first of many. It held good and bad memories of my abused daughter's father. I left him. This was when I met my husband Dave. We dated and got married. I was twenty-three.

> "And my God will meet all your needs according to the riches of his glory in Christ Jesus" (Phil. 4:19 NIV).

Chapter 7

Abusive Relationships

In my teenage years, I experienced attempted rape two times and twice as an adult, but God kept me and made a way for me to escape. My daughter's father was a very abusive man as well. My ex-boyfriend would beat me and leave me and go and party with other women and would beat them too. He had a very bad temper. When I left him about a year later, I met my husband Dave. I thought the abuse was over. Dave was a good man until we got married. Then he changed, and he was an abuser also. Dave used to chase women all weekend. Dave would start an argument with me so he could have an excuse to leave home so he could go out and party all weekend and have affairs with women. The abuse got so bad. I would hate when the weekend came because Dave would beat me up so bad, take my money, and go party it up. I got to the point that I would pay my bills before I come home, and what money I had left, Dave would take it from me and go party it up too. When Dave gave me money, he would come back and take it back from me and then would go out and party it up as well. I started going to the grocery store and bought groceries before I came home and filled my car up with gas as well before Dave came home.

I felt as if I was living for the weekend. I would go back to work mostly every Monday with black eyes, wearing sunglasses. It got to a point when I would hate when the weekend comes. I was living the same nightmare all over again weekend after weekend. I got tired of the beating, so I had him arrested and had a restraining order put on him so he could not come back. He would call me on the phone to have the restraining order taken off him. He promised he would not beat me again. Don't believe that; it was a lie. We know most abusers do not stop; either they end up killing you, or you end up killing him. If I know then what I know now, I would have left Dave long before all the abuse happened.

Don't stay in an abusive relationship. It's not going to change; it will end up getting worse. I know about silly love; it can be devastating, and with beating love, it can be failure. It seemed I was attractive to abusive men. Don't get me wrong. I did not know they were abusive until I was in the relationship with them. They would be so kind and loving at first, and as time went by, they would change.

> "But the Lord is faithful, and he will strengthen you
> and protect you from the evil one" (2 Thess. 3:3 NIV).

Chapter 8

Trying It Again

I tried the marriage again. I let Dave come back home again, and Dave did the same things again. I went to court and had a restraining order put on him. Dave left and went to Cleveland, Ohio, and kept calling and begging me to come to Cleveland and said that he would be a better husband, so I went to Cleveland, and things were good for a while. I left my two daughters with my sister in Union, South Carolina, for a little while until I got an apartment for us to stay. Dave treated me as a wife should be treated for as long as my mother was there. So I applied for a job and got the job and moved my family from Union, South Carolina, to Cleveland, Ohio. After a month, my mother, who came up with us, left and went back home; the abuse started again. I was beaten so much. I went to work with bruises and black eyes again. It had gotten so bad. My boss said to me, "You have to do something about your abusive husband, Dave, because if not, he's going to kill you one day." Well, the abuse got so bad. He beat me and threw me in the bathtub and left me there as dead and went out partying. When he came back, the blood had dried up on my face. I could not get out of the tub; I was so weak. So when Dave came back, he cleaned me up and said he was sorry and would not do it again.

That was the last draw. Dave went to sleep one day lying on the bed. I boiled a pot of hot water and went to the bed to throw the boiling water on him.

But my feet hit the bed and woke Dave up. He jumped up and ran. That was God who had my feet hit the bed because I would have gone to prison. Thanks be to God. After that, the next Friday, he came in and started arguing so he could go back out to party and be with women; I caught him with women. That Friday night I said, "Enough is enough." I was ready for Dave. I was not going to take anymore beating, so he started hitting me, and I felt in my heart that he was going to kill me that night. I reached under the bed pillow, pulled out my .22 special and started shooting (for some of you who do not know what a .22 special is, it's a gun), and Dave started running and shut the door, and the bullet went through the door and hit him in the hand and went through the hand. I opened the door, and he was still running. I don't know where he went. I called my brothers from Columbus, Ohio, and they came up to Cleveland with a U-Haul truck in a few hours and moved me and my daughters to Columbus.

> "For if you forgive other people when they sin against you, your heavenly Father will also forgive you" (Matt. 6:14 NIV)

Chapter 9

Prayer

Heavenly Father, I come to you today humbly as I know how, thanking you, Lord Jesus, for your many blessing and all you have done and are going to do in my life. I pray, God, that you will move any and everything in my path that is not righteous, and, God, cleanse me from all unrighteousness and purge me and mold me into your will and your ways and into your image. I am serving notice on you, Satan, and your demons that I am God's property. I do not belong to you, so take your hand off God's property right now in Jesus's name because you are under my feet and will remain there now and through eternity because I am covered under the blood of Jesus. God, I renounce the spirit of sickness, all fear, stress, and trauma to leave now and restore all damaged cells to normal and every hindering spirit have to go now in Jesus's name. I thank you now for keeping me when everything was looking dim in my life and when I could not see my way out. Thank you, God, for the power that moves every mountain and brings about peace and for giving me victory to continue to fight the battle of faith.

Thank you, God, for moving me out of the darkness and bringing me into the marvelous light. Thank you, God, for the light. Thank you for being my Lord of lords and King of kings in this world and the world to come. God, thank you for the door you have opened that no man can shut, and thank you for the people you are placing in my life and around me. I pray and thank you for all the distractions and hindering spirit you have moved out of my life. God, I pray for families, friends, neighbors, and coworkers to be free and delivered from their sins. I pray that chains will break off from their lives that had them bound in Jesus's name. Amen.

Chapter 10

Moved to Columbus

I moved to Columbus, Ohio, in September 1975, and my sister rented me an apartment next door to her home. My sister knew the landlord. I loved Dave so much, that crazy love. I did not have any money for the apartment, but my sisters gave me the deposit and first month's rent to get the apartment, and one of my sisters helped to pay for it, and she said to me that if I let Dave come back, I will have to pay her money back. Well, I loved him, so Dave kept on begging me to come back again, and I let him. I tried it again one more time with Dave, and the best thing happened in our marriage. I was blessed with a wonderful and handsome son. If I had to go through the trauma again, I would do it all over again for my son. My son is different from Dave. My son is a humble and a loving man who has and is doing great things for himself and his family. Oh, by the way, did I tell you Dave was off the chain here in Columbus, Ohio? He broke every marriage vow that he promised when we got married. I divorced Dave after my son was born, four months later.

Chapter 11

Near-Death Experience of Childbirth

Let me tell you that earlier when I was pregnant with my son, I had to be bedridden on the third month of my pregnancy, and throughout the whole pregnancy, I had complications. I was eight months pregnant when my father passed. We drove to Union, South Carolina. All the family and Dave went. Dave would not ride with me; he said I was too big. He just dogged me when I was pregnant as well. I was two weeks overdue. When I went into labor, my water did not break; nothing happened but bad labor pains. The umbilical cord was tied around my son's neck. He was in a breech position, so I was rushed into surgery where the doctor had to perform a C- section. I was not completely out from the anesthesia, and I saw the instrument in the doctor's hand to cut me. As I was going under the anesthesia, the doctor was saying, "Hurry! Hurry!" He said my son and I had a fifty-fifty chance to survive. Thanks be to God. I know God gave me my son because God showed me my son before he was born; he showed me he was going to be a baby boy. He showed me a big baby boy with a head full of hair, and he came out nine pounds and ten ounces, almost ten pounds, and that's the way I saw him. I bought all baby boy clothes before my baby was born. I wanted a son, and God gave me a son. God is an on- time God. Yes, he is. Dave and I divorced after my baby was born.

> "Let us therefore come boldly to the throne of grace that we may obtain mercy and find grace to help in time of need" (Heb. 4:16 NKJV).

Chapter 12

Ended the Marriage

My son was four months old when I went and filed for a divorce from Dave. He was not going to change; the same things started happening over again. I realized I had to live for my children and build a life for them and be a good mother to them. Through God's help, he strengthened me to get a job, and also through my sister's help, I survived.

I remember something my mother had said to me years ago, "If you really want to be set free from a man that is abusive and you had really given your all in all in the marriage after you have tried it all to make it work, this is what you do." When he came home from over his woman's house, I was just so kind to him. I asked Dave how his day was. Little did Dave know I had all his clothes packed in the trunk of my car, and I said to Dave, "Let us go for a joyride," and we drove around for a little while, and when I started going to the route to his woman's house, he said to me, "Where are you going?"

Dave was not going to hit me because he did not want his woman to see him act up. So I pulled to the driveway, and I went and knocked on the door, and the woman came to the door. I said to her, "Here is Dave." I went back to the car and told Dave to get out, opened the trunk, set his clothing out with him, and closed the door, and I did not look back, and I did not go back. That was the end for me, and it worked for me. Now I don't know if it would work for you, so I divorced Dave and never went back. Dave tried many times to come back, but it was over.

> "Brethren, I count not myself to have apprehended: but this one thing I do, forgetting those things which are behind, and reaching forth unto those things which are before. I press toward the mark for the prize of the high calling of God in Christ Jesus" (Phil. 3:13–14).

Chapter 13

Life-Changing Experience

When I came to Columbus, Ohio, in the late '70s, all I knew how to do was factory work at ACE sweater factory, Her Majesty clothing factory, and cotton mills/manufacturing. The first job I applied for in Columbus was custodian work, and I got the job. I was cleaning the offices at Ohio State University Hospital. I was looking at the names on the desks while I was cleaning the offices, and I said to the Lord that one day I will have my name on my office desk, and I held on to that belief that it would come to pass one day in the future. I went to work for a while at a draperies factory. I had to stop working there because the fiberglass in the draperies would break me out; I was allergic to the fiberglass, and I had to stop working there. I applied for a job at R.G. Barry Corporation, and I got the job. I worked there eight years until the shoe factory closed down. R.G. Barry gave the workers an option to go to school or take the service package or be placed into another job. Actually, I took my service-pay package and went to school at CPPI where I took secretary/word processing. And I received my secretary/word-processing diploma.

Chapter 14

Raising Three Children

It was hard raising my three children. With no help, it was a very hard past to walk, but thanks be to God and his help that I did it. My children did not have nice things like the other children, but they survived. Sometimes I would go to work sick because I could not afford to take time off from work; I could not afford health insurance. I had to work sick many days to keep a roof over our heads. We only went to the emergency room when we were so sick. We did not have a choice. The hospitals back in those days were not like they are today where you could go to the hospital and pay later. We had to use over-the-counter medicine and home remedies to heal us. Sometimes I did not have enough money to make ends meet. Thank God he was there, and I had a sister who had a grocery store. My sister gave us food from the market, and she helped me sometimes with my financial problems. I prayed to God for my children that they would not have to grow up and go through what I went through and not be poor like I was. Sometimes I had to go to bed hungry. I made sure that my children were okay.

I worked and applied for a better position on the jobs and got a promotion. I worked hard in the work field to achieve goals so my children would not have to go through life as I did. I worked two jobs at times to make ends meet. Weeping may endure for night, but joy comes in the morning.

We lived most of the time on beans, buttermilk, corn bread, and cornflakes cereal. When I applied and was blessed with a good job, thanks be to God that things got better. I was able to buy better food, and they wore better clothes, and all bills were paid.

When my children were at least fourteen, they started working for the PIC programs and bought some of their school clothing. At the age of sixteen, they got jobs working at the fast-food restaurant. By the end of their sixteenth birthdays, two of my children had their own car and license and drove themselves to school every day. All three of my children graduated and went on to be successful men and women, and the grandchildren were successful as well.

If you can hold on through the bad times and the storms, God has a bright light at the end of the tunnel. That doesn't mean you will not have other tunnels to go through. I mean you will be able to endure them and stand. We will have more disappointments to go through, but we will be able to stand and go through them together.

For my three children, I can say they did not smoke. They do drink a little but never went to jail and did no crimes. Today they are strong and powerful, successful men and women. I thank God for them. My past was an example that they would not go through the same as long as God kept breathing in my body.

> "I can do all things, through Christ who strengthens me" (Phil. 4:13 KJV).

Chapter 15

Before Coming Back to the Lord Jesus Christ

Before I rededicated my life back to Jesus Christ, I loved to shoot pool. I used to go to the bar and have a good time. I thought I was having a good time. I was the captain of the pool team. We had a winning team; we won trophies, and some of us won individual trophies for being the most valuable player. I was at the point where I was tired of going to the (bar) clubs. I started praying to God and said, "There has to be something better to life than this." I started praying and asking God to change my life. It was at a point in which I did not want to go to the club anymore, except the night I had to practice shooting pool or play in a tournament game. The other exception was when James was practicing pool for a game or playing in a tournament. I said to James that I was not coming to the club that weekend because my mom was coming over to stay for the weekend. My sisters and I took turns every weekend to keep our mother at our homes. My mother's older in age, and we had to go to Union, South Carolina, and bring her to live with us.

I picked Mother up on Friday and carried Mother back to my sister's home on Sunday evenings. James was told a lie about me. Roy kept trouble going on in the club (troublemaker).

James was told I was out all weekend with Bob. James said that I lied. Have you ever been lied on? On Monday evening after a long day at work, I went to the club to unwind and play a game of pool. When I saw James, he was so angry. He said he was told by (the liar) Roy that I was out with another man all weekend long. Have you ever tried to explain to a person that you are not lying and they did not believe you? I tried to explain to James that I was at home all weekend with my mother as I said to him I would be. With James's jealous rage, James ended up losing his temper and life over a lie that was told by Roy.

James went and approached Bob, the man I supposedly had been out with all weekend (lies). Bob, who was accused, spoke to James and said that it was not true as well. It led to a big argument, and I saw James pull out a knife, and Bob had a gun. I watched them both as I was shooting pool. Then Bob told James, "Let us take this outside." James walked out the door first, and I stopped shooting pool and walked out behind James, and then Bob walked out behind me and started shooting and hit James in the leg. James fell to the ground, and as he was getting back up, Bob walked over to James and stood over him and shot James in the head two times.

The devil has come to steal, kill, and destroy, but Jesus has come for us to have life and have it more abundantly.

Then Bob turned and looked at me and walked over to me, and I went down on my knees and called on the name of Jesus, and Bob turned around and walked back into the club. I got in my car. I was in a state of shock. I don't know how I made it home, but I do know it was God who saved me. I cried and called on the name of Jesus all the way home. On January 20, 1989, when I woke up the next morning, I became a new creature in Jesus Christ. Old things were gone, and things became new. God took the old lifestyle away (the old woman) overnight. I never drank alcohol again and never went to the (bar) club again. The things I used to do were in the past. I was in a state of mind where I did not know what to do all week long. It seemed as if my head was going to explode out of my body. On January 24, 1989, I was walking in the house from my living room to the kitchen back and forth, and I began to cry out loud to God. I was walking by my refrigerator, and I heard a voice, and I looked up over the top of my refrigerator. I heard a voice say to me, "If you make one step, I would make two." I knew who the voice was; it Jesus Christ. I felt as if I was in a straitjacket bound from head to foot. Jesus came in and touched me and healed me. It was the way I was feeling. No one could have given me peace but God. I was so broken. I could not do anything but yield myself to Jesus; that was all I wanted to do. My life started changing. I started going back to church faithfully every Sunday and did Bible study, and every time we had some type of services at church, I was there.

> "Let your roots grow down into him, and let your lives be built on him. Then your faith will grow strong in the truth you were taught, and you will overflow with thankfulness" (Col. 2:7 NLT).

Chapter 16

Never Say Never on What You Are Going to Do

I said to the God that I was going to give my life back to him, and I was giving God a time limit. I was coming back to him to be saved in a few months. God said, "No, you're coming back now." I know now that when God means now, he means now. I know now that God was pruning me for a time such as this. The things I used to do went away overnight. Revival at my church started in March 1989, and I went to revival every night. On Wednesday night, Pastor G was preaching, and one of the mothers, Marie, said to me, "Are you saved?"

I said, "I am a backslider."

And she said, "You are the one Pastor G was preaching about tonight." I felt so bad. I had spoken to God, and I said I was coming back to him in a few months. How could I tell God anything? He was in control. I was not in a position to tell God anything but to save me.

Mother Marie knew what she was talking about. Mother Marie was a very wise mother (of the church). You could not fool her and the old wise mothers of the church back then. Pastor G was preaching about the backslider coming back home to Jesus Christ, and that Thursday night, things were happening when Pastor G preached. I could hardly maintain myself. There was a voice that said to me, "You don't want to go up there," and it gave me all kinds of reasons why I should not go up there and accept Jesus Christ.

I said, "You are wrong, devil." I was wrong for listening to him. I did not go up to give my life to Jesus Christ that night. I was still a backslider.

When I got in my car, I cried. I sat there for a few minutes thinking on what I should have done. I was so convicted that I went back into the church, and everyone that could help me was gone. I got back in my car and cried all the way home, and I said to the Lord, "Sit in front of my apartment. Just give me one more day and one more chance. I am coming back home to you tomorrow night (which was Friday night)." The next morning when I got up, all kinds of things were happening to keep me from getting to church that Friday night. I had promised my sister that I would pick her up and bring her to church with me. I picked up my sister in my car, and we were going across the railroad tracks, and I got a pressing pain in my chest. It was pressing down in my chest so severe that it felt as if I was having a heart attack. I was holding my chest and breathing so hard. My sister said to me, "Maybe you need to go to the hospital."

I said, "No, because I am going on to church." And I started praying and saying the blood of Jesus. I said, "Get behind me, Satan, in the name of Jesus. I know what you are trying to do." Satan was trying to stop the process of me returning back to God. I was focused on God. "No weapon formed against me shall prosper. It won't work."

My sister was not saved, and she could not understand what I was saying. My sister said, "What are you saying 'Get behind me, Satan, in the name of Jesus' for?"

Then I said to my sister, "I am going to be all right." The devil was trying to stop us from getting to church that Friday night because of what I had said to Jesus Christ the night before. Devil was on his mission, but God had the solution and plan for my soul, and God prevailed. When we got to church and started walking down the sidewalk to the church, there was a shaggy grayish-black dog. It walked in the church beside me. It was talking to me, trying to discourage me from giving my life to Jesus Christ that night. Satan knew in his mind I was going down in front that Friday night to answer the call and rededicate my life back to my Lord and Savior Jesus Christ. The evil spirit in the dog was saying, "You know you don't need to go down there. You're okay." The dog was sitting on the floor beside my seat; I had an aisle seat, and the demon in the dog who was sitting on the floor by my seat was talking all throughout the service trying to convince me not to go up to the altar.

When Pastor G gave the signal for the altar call, I went down in front and received the Lord Jesus Christ back into my life as my personal Lord and Savior, no longer a backslider. I looked back, and the dog was walking out of the church door with his tail tucked between it legs. The dog (demon) was walking as if it knew it had lost the battle. *The battle is not yours; it is the Lord's.*

> The Spirit of the Sovereign Lord is upon me, for the Lord anointed me to bring good news to the poor. He has sent me to comfort the brokenhearted and to proclaim that captives will be released and prisoners will be freed. He has sent me to tell those who mourn that the time of the Lord's favor has come, and with

it, the day of God's anger against their enemies. To all who mourn in Israel, he will give a crown of beauty for ashes, a joyous blessing instead of mourning, festive praise instead of despair. In their righteousness, they will be like great oaks that the Lord has planted for his own glory. (Isa. 6:1–3 NLT)

… Chapter 17

Testimony No. 1

I was giving a testimony on the last night of revival, and I looked out over the congregation, talking to the crowd of people in church, and I saw what came over the sanctuary. It was filled with fog; the only thing I could see was fog. When I came down in the spirit, the church (saints) was up on their feet praising, shouting, and crying. They were giving God the glory for what he has done. I was told by a few members from the visiting church that God was going to use me for his work and glory. That was nothing but God who used them to give me that word. I was changed. Never tell the Lord what you are going to do, but I learned quickly: God is in control, not

I. After that night of receiving Jesus Christ back into my life, I was put through test after test, and I had to pass every test that was put before me by God to see if I was going to be strong enough to stand and endeavor the tests. All the tests that I had to go through started with family, friends, and the bar friends, and I stood through the trials. I passed the tests Jesus ordered and told me to carry out. I did it. The last test was a test with a check, and I passed the test.

Love, strength, and butterfly.

Chapter 18

Testimony No. 2

The test was with a check. I went to the corner store where I would go to cash my check. The store clerk cashed the $34 and some change. I asked the store clerk for a money order. He gave me the money order I requested and the $34 and change and the cash back from the check and did not charge me for the money order. When I got to the car, I looked at the money order and the amount of money that I gave to the store clerk. It was correct. The clerk had given me the same amount of money back for the check of $34 and change. So I left with the cash and money order. I went out to my sister's store, told my sister what had happened, and she looked at me and said, "What are you going to do?" My sister spoke these words; she said to me to follow my heart.

Then my brother came in the store. I told him what had happened. He said to me, "Well, you have not stolen the money, so I would keep the money." Of course, he would say that. My brother was not saved. After a few minutes, I went back to the store and told the store clerk what he had done. The store clerk thanked me. He said some people would not have been earnest enough to bring the money back to the store. I said to the store clerk that if this had happened a few months ago, I would not have been earnest enough to bring it back either. I thanked God for putting me through the test to see if I could stand against temptation.

> "Your word is a lamp unto my feet and light unto my path" (Ps. 119:103).

The last thing I experienced was I had a dream. I kept on dreaming about newborn babies. I went out to my sister's home the next day, which was Labor Day. I asked my sister why I was dreaming about newborn babies. I said, "Does that mean I'm being born again?" When I said that, there was a feeling that came through my body. I'd never felt that way before. It was so awesome, powerful, and I was strengthened.

My sister started shouting, "Of course!" She was the saved sister with the right information when I asked. I thanked God for my sister's prayer. She kept on praying for me when I wanted my sister to stop praying, but she was persistent in praying, working on me to come back to the Lord.

My sister called. I would not take her telephone calls. I would tell the children to tell her I was not home, but she heard me say to my children through the phone that I was not there; she heard my voice. You know how telephones were back in the '80s; with the three-party telephone lines, everyone could hear when everyone calls. My sister would get in the car and drive over to my apartment. She did not give up on me. I am so thankful today that my sister did not give up on me. She can tell my mother up there in heaven that she did not give up on me.

I thank God that my sister did not give up on me. Today in this age, family members will get upset when you talk to them about Jesus.

Most families will get upset because they want to do their own thing, but we as kingdom servants have to tell our family and people about Jesus who saves. I understand when family gets upset with us because I am one of those who talks to my family to come to Jesus. I used to say the same thing, "Just leave me alone. I am not ready." I was a backslider. It was hard for me to come back, but thanks be to God for a persistent sister and the bodies of Jesus Christ who love talking to the lost soul about salvation in Jesus Christ. When family members want to be left alone, we still need to pray for them. Family, do not stop praying, whether they like it or not. Keep praying. Do not give up on your family because God did not give up on me, and he will not give up on you. Love your family even when they don't love you back.

> "For God so love this world that He gave his only begotten son that whosoever believe in him should not perish, but shall have everlasting [eternal] life" (John 3:16).

Chapter 19

Dreaming of Marriage

I remarried about twenty years later, and I saw my husband in a dream. Well, I was given a choice. There were three men in my dream, and all three were sitting on high-back chairs that swirl around. I asked each one of them to say something to me, and they did and swirled around in the high-back chair. I listened to each one of them. Then I said that one is to be my husband. I know I chose the wrong one. I was looking at him. He was tall, handsome, had curly black hair and a nice build. Well, he was a man in disguise. He presented himself to be a man that loved God as much as I did. He deceived me as a husband and a man to set the example of being a leader over my family and the church. I had some good days and most bad days with him, and the bad outweighed the good.

Chapter 20

Running from the Calling

God had called me into the ministry in 1992. I heard his voice, and I ran from God. One day, Mike said that God has called me to the ministry, and I was running from God. I knew it was God telling Mike that. God had spoken those same words to me, and I ignored his voice. Then one day, God's voice came to me again. He said, "I have called you to myself."

I said, "Lord, I like what I am doing. I am an usher, and I like it." I was asked by the chief usher to take his place because he was going to step down. I said that I was happy being an usher. I was a great usher. I liked what I was doing.

God said to me, "You have gone as far as you can to go here at this church. I have called you to the ministry to help reach my peoples." God knew that I have a heart for people. I did not understand then what he meant, but I know now to the fullest. My mission is to reach the lost souls and evangelize God's word to the broken, hurting, sick, lost, to bring healing, deliverance, and to set the captives free.

> "If any of you lacks wisdom, you should ask God, who gives generously to all without finding fault, and it will be given to you" (James 1:5 NIV).

Chapter 21

Hurt Beyond Measure

When I got married to husband no. 2, Mike, it was good at first. There were some little things I overlooked. I thought in time they would go away. Mike always had women around him. When we started our church ministry, we opened up a prophetic ministry. Mike was the pastor and the prophet. We worked well together. Then in our marriage, all things started breaking apart, causing the marriage to go to the lowest level, hurting because of the women he picked up and brought to church. Mike would not let me pick up the women. There came all types of infidelity, lies, and deceit, things I had experienced and seen. We could never go out of town alone together. Mike always had Jill with us and said it was all right. I will tell the rest on that story later on. I thought I was hurt with my first husband, Dave, but oh my god, Mike was a mental abuser.

I think that I would rather be beaten any day than to go through mental abuse. It is devastating. It messes with your mind. It's a hurt that does not go away but only through God and his timing. Physical beatings go away in a few days, but the pain in mental abuse lingers. Did you know that if you get hit upside your head so many times it will cause severe problems in your head in the future? Mental abuse tears you down. You cannot think properly. It comes with depression, causes eating disorders; you eat just to fill the empty part in you, but actually there is still an empty void inside. All parts of the body want to do their own things, which is to shut down, lose faith, and die. God can bring us through it all.

> "I can do all things through Christ who strengthens me" (Phil. 4:13).

With the hurt of abuse, you sometimes do things that you don't realize you have done. The hurt and pain is so severe. It's as if a knife was stuck in your stomach and twisted it around until there was nothing left but a shell. When we get married, sometimes think that we can change our spouse. Be wise. If you see that problem before marrying him, it's not going to change afterward. Sometimes as humans we go into a marriage thinking that we can change a person. That is far from the truth. We can only change ourselves; leave the change up to God to do because he is the only one who can change a person. I give thanks to God that I was saved when I went into this marriage. God taught me how to hold my peace, how he would fight my battles.

Mike loved women. He was always around women after we get to the church. As if one man or person could run the church alone, he did everything except clean the bathroom; that was something I did all the time, taking care of all the cleaning. I thanked God I could do so as a humble service unto the Lord. After the church was up and running, we had members. Mike suggested I drive myself to church. He would go pick up women and bring them to church. I was not a jealous wife because I was anchored in the Lord. He knew I was not going to cheat on him. Mike told me that one of the men who came to church told him I would not cheat on him. That was the truth. I did not believe in that lifestyle. I am to be a holy woman before God and loyal to my husband.

> "Beloved, do not avenge yourselves, but rather give place to wrath, for it is written, 'Vengeance is mine, I will repay,' says the Lord."

Sometimes a husband (man) will take their wife or girlfriend for granted when they know they have a good wife, and it's the same thing for the wife; she will do the same to their husband as well. Mike got to the point where he would not let me ride with him to church. Mike would go pick up Jill from her home and bring Jill to church. Mike would never pick up men and bring them to church. In all church services, Mike would make me drive to church in town and sometimes in out-of-town church services. I found out later that Mike was having affairs with most of the women he was picking up and bringing to church. God revealed to me the affairs of some of them. I asked Mike about them; he denied it and became angry with me. Jill, who caused me so many problems, broke up my home. We separated. Jill, whom Mike was having an affair with, talked Mike into divorcing me. Jill wanted Mike for her husband. Oh, by the way, Mike married Jill about a year later after we divorced. Look at this. Mike did not have grounds to divorce me. Mike made up some lies and said we were incompatible, but in the beginning, we were. Mike did not have an attorney; he was his own attorney. Did I not say Jill wanted Mike so bad that she coached him into divorcing me? We made a vow to each other that we would not divorce each other. How quickly Mike forgot the vows, among other things.

As the church started growing, Mike started disrespecting me by not acknowledging me and started acknowledging Jill. Mike was having an affair with Jill. They were seen out in a restaurant and on a cookout on a holiday together. Mike would not spend holiday time with me or on special days or events. The first time I saw Jill, I knew she was trouble. We were at a revival. Jill was doing praise and worship. She kept looking at Mike. After praise and worship, Jill sat in the seat in front of Mike, slung her hair in his face. She kept on doing this to be noticed by Mike.

I knew from that night Jill was a problem, and I was right. The Holy Spirit revealed it to me. Jill said that she wanted to get to know us and that she wanted to be friends with us. Jill said that Mike preached a good message and that she would like to call to talk to us and come to our church sometime. She called. She said she wanted to be our friend and asked if Mike was home. I said *no*. Jill called back later, asked to talk to Mike a few more times, so Jill stopped calling me. She waited until Mike came home, never talking with me again until she was in court with Mike at our divorce hearing.

(God says in the Word to never put his wife or husband away without good cause.)

Chapter 22

Church Deception

The spirit of Jezebel came into the church and ripped the church apart. I know Mike was calling Jill. Jill said to Mike that they had churches she wanted him to come preach. Well, we went and preached. It did not end there though. The next thing I knew, Mike was going to a meeting that Jill was having at their church. He started talking about how she was going to get him set up in one of their churches. One of Mike's women called our home, and I asked who was calling. She would not tell me; she hung up on me. I asked Mike who she was since she did not give me a name. Mike got angry because I asked him who the woman was. He said to me that he is getting himself a separate telephone line and have it put in his bedroom, and he did so. That woman brought so much hurt and deception to our home, to our marriage. Mike let Jill destroy our home as well. Almost every service we had at church, Mike would go pick up Jill and bring her to church services. The only time Jill was not at service was when she did not have service at their church. Mike rarely took me anywhere with him. When we went out of town to a church summit in Georgia or any function, Jill was in the car in the back seat. At the church summit, Mike sat with Jill and had me to sit somewhere else alone. If I only knew then what I know now, things would have been different.

> God says, "But I will not have you to be ignorant brethren, concerning them which are asleep, that ye sorrow not, even as others which have no hope" (1 Thess. 4:13).

Chapter 23

Separation in the Home

We were separated at home, everything from the bedroom to the kitchen appliances, bathrooms, computers, cars, bank accounts, house telephones. We had nothing together but hurt and pain. We could not go on vacation together; Jill would be there. When we went to church functions, Jill would always be in the car in the back seat and sat behind Mike. They looked back and forth at each other through the mirror. Do you know what pain I was in and going through? But God kept me clothed in my right mind. When I said *separations in the home*, we were divided; we had two of everything. God kept me in my right mind because I kept my mind staying on him. If not, I could not have withstood what I went through. When we were on our way back from Georgia after attending a weekend summit, Mike got mad at me and said that he will never be going to bring me back to Georgia or anywhere else with him again. I did not know what his reason was, and I did not ask. As we were driving, I started writing down the route to Georgia, and Mike got mad, pulled the car over, took my notebook, tore the pages out, threw them out the window on the highway, and grabbing my hands, he said, "I curse these hands so you cannot use to write with them again." Jill was smirking at me. I was praying to God it won't happen so I will be able to use my hands and will be able to continue using my hands and all my limbs. Well, these hands wrote this book, and I will do many more things with my hands. God gave these hands to me, and only he can take them away from me, as what the Lord says.

> I say to those with fearful hearts, "Be strong, and do not fear, for your God is coming to destroy your enemies. He is coming to save you" (Isa. 35:4 NLKT).

Chapter 24

Loss of Church Memberships

I can go on and on. It got so bad that the members started leaving the church. They said that they could not sit by and look at how Mike was treating me any longer. Mike would not let my granddaughter come to stay the night or weekend with me any longer. I watched my granddaughter every weekend for my daughter. At that time, she worked on Sundays. My granddaughter would go to church with me every Sunday. After Mike and I got married, Mike stopped my granddaughter and daughters from coming to our home. He did not want any of my family to come over. My son came home from the navy for a week. He had driven twelve hours from Virginia Beach, Virginia. He was tired and sleepy. Mike said to me, "Your son cannot stay here." Mike said for me to tell him that he could not stay.

I said, "I will not. You have to tell him yourself." Mike waited up in his bedroom for hours until my son came home at two o'clock in the morning. Mike came downstairs and told my son that he could not stay and that he had to leave. My son never did anything but had respect for Mike. My son always said, "Yes, sir." He said he will leave. My son respected Mike. Then he left. I went with my son. My daughter lived a few streets over from us, so my son and I went to my daughter's home. Mike was so mean that he broke up twenty-five years of friendship with one of my girlfriends and me. We established our friendship back. We had the love of Jesus in our hearts and knew the love of having family. Sometimes when people don't have children themselves, they don't know the love of children. I am not saying this about all people. You know what type of fruit you are bearing. I am just saying that you don't know the pain I carry for the oil in this alabaster box.

> "The thief comes only to steal and kill and destroy; I have come that they may have life, and have it to the full" (John 10:10 NIV).

Chapter 25

Spent Time from Home

Mike would spend all holidays away from home. He would leave in the morning and would not come back home until night. Mike was seen with Jill at her family cookout. Every function Jill had, he was there. Mike would drive forty-five minutes to a small city and pick Jill up for church service and then bring her back home after service. If I was in the car, Mike would take Jill over to her daughter's home so I would not now where Jill lived. Like I said, it was rare that I would be in the car with Mike alone. I asked Mike if he was having an affair with Jill. He said *no*. What a lie that was. I knew Mike was having an affair with Jill; the Holy Spirit revealed it to me, just as what the Holy Spirit revealed to me when Mike got mad at me and took Jill on my ten-day vacation and conference. He told everyone at the conference that Jill was his wife. When the Holy Spirit spoke to me, I got upset. The Holy Spirit said that Mike had Jill with him. That was a hurting thing for Mike to do to me—spend my vacation on Jill, the jezebel, who broke up our home and marriage and broke up other women's marriages. She caused so much problems, hurt, and pain to me and others.

I called Mike and begged him to let me come; it was when he was on a vacation and conference. He said no, using excuses, lies, etc., knowing he had taken Jill instead of me. When Mike came back home that following Sunday, I was from a church service when I got home that night. Mike was lying in bed trying to be so nice, as if he wanted to be with me. Stop the madness! He was so nice; it was sickening to me. I knew something was up. He knew I was a smart woman. Mike started telling me what things the Holy Spirit had already revealed to me. Mike knew I was going to know about them anyway.

We were to go together to Georgia on vacation and to the conference. Mike said that he took Jill with him on vacation and to the conference in Georgia. I went in a rage and started hitting my head against the wall until I passed out. When I came to my consciousness, Mike was on the telephone with the apostle from the church conference we were going to. Mike took Jill instead of me, his wife. Can you imagine how he explained that one? Mike was caught up in lies to the apostle.

Mike told the apostle I had died and that he brought me back to life. The apostle asked Mike, "What happened? Your wife and you were fine when you were here." Mike had to tell the apostle from Georgia that Jill was not his wife. Oh, can you imagine what happened next? A few months later, we went back to Georgia to a summit to the church that Mike had taken Jill to church service, conference. The apostles wanted to see me, the real wife. So when we walked in the church, the church ministry said, "How are you, Elder Mike and Minister B?"

Mike then looked at me, and the elder said, "Oh, you are not the wife Elder Mike had with him the last time he was here."

I said, "I am Elder Mike's wife." It was an uproar in the church.

I thank God for his mercy. You can lie, but you cannot hide when you're touching God-anointed ones. Hallelujah. I was angry, but I sinned not.

> "In your anger do not sin: Do not let the sun go down while you are still angry, and do not give the devil a foothold" (Eph. 4:26–27 NIV).

Chapter 26

Awake—Accident in Dream before It Happened

I had a dream about my grandson. Paul was walking with me down the road near an overhead bridge on the east side. Down below was a road. I was walking down the hill to the road, and Paul was walking down the hill too close to the edge of the road. Paul fell down in the oncoming traffic. I ran down the hill after him. When I got to Paul, there were so many people around him. I had to ask them to move so I could get to Paul. Paul was not breathing. He had a knot on his forehead, a knot on the back of his neck, and a knot on the bottom of his lower back. The emergency squad was still trying to revive Paul. I said, "What am I going to tell Candy [Paul's mother]?" So the emergency squad continued to work on Paul, but they could not revive him, and the emergency squad stopped working on Paul.

Then the Holy Spirit said to me to continue to pray for Paul, start laying hands on him, pray and start anointing Paul from head to toe, and go up and down his body three times. I did what the Holy Spirit said. Then breath came back into his body. Paul sat up, looked at me, got up, and started walking around as if nothing had happened.

I told Candy about the dream. I also said that it did not mean it had to be Paul; it could be another one of our family members or friend or someone else we know.

Well, about two weeks later, Candy called me screaming and howling out loud. She said that my niece's son had been hit by a COTA bus on the crosswalk and was taken to the hospital. I asked Candy what hospital he was in. I would like to go see Joe. Joe was kept in the hospital overnight for observation. Joe had a head concussion, knot on the forehead, a knot on back of his neck, and a knot on the lower bottom of his back. The hospital relieved him the next day to go home. I called my niece and asked her if I could go visit Joe. She said, "Yes, you can go visit Joe." I had Bible study that Wednesday night, so I said to my niece that I would stop by after Bible study. After Bible study was over, I prepared myself to go to my nephew Joe's apartment. I heard a voice saying, "You are tired. You need to go home and rest."

Then I said, "Maybe I do need to rest." I was listening to that voice.

Then I heard another voice say, "You need to go visit Joe. He needs you." Then I told Satan to get behind me in the name of Jesus.

When I got to Joe's apartment, Joe was lying down. He was in pain. He appeared the same way as I saw him in the dream. Joe had a knot on his forehead. I said to him, "You have a knot on your neck too and a knot at the lower bottom of your back." Then Joe looked at me, amazed. The Holy Spirit started talking to me again to anoint Joe down with oil from his head to his toes, lay hands on him, go up and down his body three times, and speak healing over his body. After laying hands and praying for Joe, I went up and down his body as I was instructed in the dream. Joe got up, started running around the room, shouting, "I am healed," and started playing with the children in their apartment. Thanks be to God for the Holy Spirit, and being obedient to the Holy Spirit, Joe was healed.

Chapter 27

Move Out of the Problems

I was talking to God saying that I could not take it anymore. When doors would open up for me, I would get an apartment. Don't tell me that God wants to move you out of the problems that are not lined up with his word in your life, as what Mike was doing to me. When you have done everything to stand, yes, he will move you out of issues that no one can move or get you out of but God.

God moved me out of the problems. I went and looked for an apartment to be separated from Mike. After applying for the apartment, I was told at the rental office that another person had put the deposit down on that apartment. So I said to the manager, "If that apartment is for me, the application will not go through." The manager said to me to call back in a few days to see if they had any other apartment available for rent.

The apartment manager called me back in two days and said, "Ms. B, the apartment is yours if you still want it. The application of the other person did not go through."

When God has his hands on you, nobody can do anything to you no matter how hard they try.

So after God had brought things to pass with getting the apartment for me, I did not want to leave Mike, but God knew what was best for me. I could not take the mental abuse anymore. I was making excuses to stay with Mike. God let me know it was time for me to go. Thank God, I listened to his voice. I went on and accepted the apartment. Oh yes, I had all kinds of grounds for divorce. I said that I didn't do anything, so if Mike wanted a divorce from me, he would have to file. Jill talked Mike into getting a divorce with no grounds. That's how badly Jill wanted my husband for herself.

Mike drove Jill around everywhere she wanted to go. Mike had Jill in the car so much that her butt print was in the seat, and that's no lie.

Mike wouldn't support me on anything I was doing or planning, but he would go to Jill and support her in everything she was doing. I was so miserable in my home but not at first. After all the problems occurred, it was like looking out of the windows of my home as if they had bars on the windows. I felt as if I was in prison in my own home. Although I could not see the bars outside, I could feel them.

I saw myself look out the window. I was bound up in it. I felt as if I was in a nightmare waiting to wake up. I'd never been to prison if prison was worth than what I lived in and went through. I am never going to that place. I was closed in from my family, friends, and they could not come to my home. Mike did not want to have company. Mike did not want anyone to come to the home. I was not used to that. I was raised with a family, a big family at that, where I knew how to love and show love to others. Like I said, it was not like that at first. I enjoyed Mike because he was good to me.

If Mike could have put his flesh under subject, among other issues, we could have had a good marriage.

> "Whether you turn to the right or to the left, your ears will hear a voice behind you, saying, 'This is the way; walk in it'" (Isa. 30:21 NIV).

There was a time when I was married to Mike that ACS heard about my husband and had gotten into an argument, and he physically touched me in an abusive way, and I left him and went and stayed with my daughter. ACS said that if I went back to him again, ACS would never talk to me again. I went back to Mike again. ACS said that he would cut himself off from me, and he did. ACS's girlfriend kept me informed on how ACS was doing. So I prayed and talked to the Lord. The Lord told me to fast for three days with no water, no food, and I did what the Lord told me to do. It was so hard; it was the hardest fast I ever went on. In the last few hours, I was so weak. It was as if it was not going to happen. I was down to the last two hours before my fast ended. It was as God said. I would hear from ACS. About two hours before my fast ended, I got a call from ACS, and he apologized to me. It was hard for both of us to be apart from each other and not talk to each other for a period of time because we had a close relationship.

My children are so protective of me. God brought me through. If I keep the faith and stay on the path to God and listen to his voice, all things shall come to pass as God said it will.

After going through all the things I went through in marriage, I had to go into quiet time with God. I took a shower and anointed myself down with anointed oil and dressed in white apparel from my head to my feet in white linen. I placed the white linen on the floor, went into the chamber to meet the bridegroom, shut out everything, and lay before God for a few hours. Power and anointment came over me in a way I had never experienced before.

> "Thou word is a lamp unto my feet and a light unto my pass" (Ps. 119:105).

Chapter 28

Only God Can Put Pieces Back Together

After our home separation and divorce, I was so broken. I was as a bird with two broken wings; I couldn't fly. I was stressed, fearful, angry, bitter, and depressed. I ended up getting so sick. I had to have treatment for my conditions, but the treatment was not doing me any good. I called my doctor's office, and the nurse said that I could not get an appointment until after a month. I told the nurse that I could not wait a month. I lay on my bed in so much pain. My daughter called, and I could hardly move. She told me she would call me right back. My daughter went to my surgeon. They worked together in the OR. She told him what happened. My doctor told her to tell me to come in through the emergency room. I ended up in the hospital to have a major surgery. I had to build up my body one week before the doctor could do surgery on me. It was that bad. My entire family was called to come to the hospital before I went to surgery. The doctor told my family that I might not make it. That was true. I died on the operating table for twenty minutes. While I was dead, I saw a glimpse of heaven; I saw Jesus. He was standing in front of the choir; they were getting ready to sing. As far as I could see were the choir of people or (angel) and Jesus. Jesus looked at me and pointed at me and the choir stand. There was only one place left on the choir.

I went and stood with the choir. When I looked again, I had on a big wide hat. Everything was so beautiful. I felt no pains. I was saying to Jesus I did not want to go back. I felt so good and at peace. Before the surgery, I prayed to Jesus to come back to this world to be with my family. I said that they needed me. Yet after seeing heaven, I did not want to return to this world. Jesus said to me, "It's not your time yet. You have work to do." So Jesus said I have to go back. So I dropped back into my body with all the pain. I was hurting so bad. I could not stand it. That was the first time I was given morphine for pain. I said to God that it's so beautiful here in heaven. I did not want to come back here to this world. God sent me back to finish my work here in this world. I have to finish what Jesus has called me to do to help build his kingdom so God can be well pleased and glorified with me.

> "Finally, be strong in the Lord and in his mighty power. Put on the full armor of God, so that you can take your stand against the devil's schemes" (Eph. 6:10–11 NIV).

Chapter 29

Going through Divorce Causes Pain

When going through a divorce, it is like death; you lose part of your ribs. God took a rib out of Adam and made woman. When you are married, you become one, "bone of my bone and flesh of my flesh." I don't understand how men and women can easily jump out of a marriage unless they were not in love with each other in the first place or if it was not for the right reasons. Let me tell you what happened to me when I was divorced for the wrong reasons. Mike did not have grounds to divorce me. Mike and Jill made up something, and we got a divorce. If you read up in Corinthians on what Jesus said about divorce, with what Mike did, he had no reason to divorce me. Jesus also said that if you put your wife away without causes, you are not free to marry again. There are so many men and women putting their spouse away for the wrong reason. If we get married for the right reason and we divorce, it will hurt as if it was like death. You will go through grief, hurt, and pain. You can only endure when that bone is broken apart. Have you ever had any bone broken apart? Then you know how bad it hurts until it heals. That was the way I felt when those bones came apart in a divorce.

Chapter 30

Divorce Leaves Grief

This is my story. I was messed up for ten years with grief and loss. I was broken into so many fragments. Only God could put them back together again.

I had to let go of the hurt and pain I was carrying. I was broken. I went through hurt, pain, bitterness, and rejection. I was not growing in the ministry as I should. So much hurt was stacked on my spirit. My spirit was buried under a pile of stuff that was hurting me with pain and rejection. I could not function as a whole person. Stuff were stacked up, buried in me for ten years. I kept praying and talking to the Lord God for relief. I kept on seeking God, and things started getting better for me. I talked to other married couples who experienced marriage problems for advice as well. I received some relief in training-class setting when God gave one of the teachers (minister) a word of prophecy spoken over me; it helped me as well. One day I said, "Lord, show me what I need to do." I talked to an elder of our church and asked her to mentor me. I had one session with her, and through that session, she said I had to take off all those layers of hurt, pain, rejection, and distraction and let God in and heal me. That was the answer—purge out all the stuff that had me buried, so I called out all those things and was healed. My strength came back; the ministry came back to me strong and powerful. My authority on anointing was stronger. I thank God for my relief and breakthrough.

> Now may our Lord Jesus Christ Himself and God our Father, Who loved us and gave us everlasting consolation and encouragement and well-founded hope through [His] grace (unmerited favor). Comfort and encourage your hearts and strengthen them [make them steadfast and keep them unswerving] in every good work and word. (2 Thess. 2:16–17 AMPC)

Chapter 31

Can We Be Bound Up and Not Know It?

Sometimes we can be bound up and not know that we are bound. I was so unhappy. Sometimes we can have so much stuff on us until it takes some time for us to be healed. It took ten years for me to be healed and delivered. We can carry so much stuff packed up on the inside, such as anger, bitterness, hatred, rage, hurt, rejection, depression, stress, and pain, until we can't hear the Holy Spirit talking to us. We as Christians have to relieve the load and burden and turn it over to God. I do not have a problem with forgiveness. No matter how bad I am hurt, I have to forgive, let go, and let God be my all in my life. Does that make sense? I thank God for releasing me from things that I went through and endured. I thank God for my spiritual mom who adopted me as her daughter in 2005, Pastor M.

When I was so sick in the hospital and died on the operating table and Jesus brought me back to life, Pastor M was there for me day and night. She would come over to my apartment and stay with me for hours. I could call her at any time at home, and she would be there for me. Pastor M was there when both my wings were broken. I could not fly. I was broken in so many fragments. They were small as glitters. I could see myself as such glitters. God put all the pieces back together, filled the broken place, and joined the broken pieces back together in its proper places. I thank God for closing this chapter in my life and opened up a new one. I am writing a new chapter, new beginning, and God who is the head of my life gets the glory, he who controls and gives us the increase. I had to go through things in my life to get where God would have me to walk, see the visions, dream dreams, and the calling and plans God has for my life.

Chapter 32

Jesus Will Put Our Life in Perspective

Through Jesus Christ, my life was put back together after all the abuse. In 2004, after the separation, I did not think I could go on with life. I was so broken as a bird with two broken wings. I did not have any energy or strength to move forward. I felt I was not going to make it through this time. I felt I could not get myself back together again. I was so broken that when I looked at myself, everything in my life was broken in fragments; every piece of me was in so many little fragments. I felt as if I could not be put back together again. I said to Pastor M that I didn't think I was going to make it this time. I was so broken. I did not think I was going to pull through. Pastor M said, "Yes, you will come through this. God will bring you through." I said I didn't know about this, this time. The pain was not like any other I had experienced. I can feel the pain all the way through my bones. Like I said, marriage and divorce is like death, your rib breaking apart from one another. If you had broken ribs, you know how it feels, and worse is when the other rib is broken away.

It was so hard for me to bear it. It hurt so bad. Everything was hurting, and I could just see myself in little fragmented pieces; they were so small. I could barely see them. In my spirit, I was so broke, and in my heart, I could not endure the pain. God came in and put the broken pieces back together from the hurt and pain of my divorce. I was so stressed out, hurt, angry, and depressed. I could not think straight. Things were so bad for me that it affected my ministry, my work, and my life. I ended up getting so sick with problems going on in my body. Within a year's time, I had let all the symptoms in my body take down a spiral turn. Not once did I give up on God. It just seemed in my mind like he was not there. I did not know whether the Holy Spirit was present in my life or not. God was there when I was in such a state of mind. I did not know and could not hear his voice. I was still going to church and praised God. I still felt lost. Pastor M would call me every day, if it was possible, for encouragement and prayer.

I could call Pastor M anytime day or night to talk to her. What if she was like some pastors today who stopped taking calls after a sudden hour at night? I will not shut off my telephone at any time at night. My door is always open to everyone who has a problem and needs my help. Do not call if you have a broken nail and needs to talk.

I thank God for strong friends and spiritual mother Pastor M whom God placed in my life when I was going through separation and marriage, breakup, and divorce. When I felt I was finished (at the point of giving up), God started little by little in putting the fragment pieces back together again. It took me ten years to fully recover. God taught me how to pull up and how to crawl and how to make baby steps and how to walk and how to run again.

I started running for Jesus in a way I did not think was possible; it was a long process. I learned how to do all things again through Jesus Christ who strengthened me. The Holy Spirit taught me how to depend on him. He was there holding me up when I was hurting so badly. He was wrapping every tear when I was learning how to pull up. He was there at every side making sure I would be able to balance, stand, and with his hand, he held me. During my baby steps, Jesus was there to keep me from falling. My eyes were open in the spirit. I could not see that far in the spirit because Mike broke his vows and left me hurting as a bird with broken wings. The Holy Spirit kept nursing me back to health, physically, mentally, emotionally, and spiritually. God broke every chain of my life that had me bound. I am here to tell you that mental abuse is worse than physical abuse, but God can heal it.

Let me tell you something. Please listen to what I am saying. If you have not gone through abuse, you have an option not to get into that situation. Well, let me tell you; you know you are free when you can talk about the hurt, pain, sickness, depression, and the abuse.

I was waiting for that day when I would see Mike again, how I would react or handle it. Hear what happened to me when I was up and running again. I became a new creation from all hurt, bitterness, disappointment, and pain. I had already forgiven Mike and Jill. I love God too much to hold onto unforgiveness. It was not easy, but through Christ I can do all things. I was anticipating the day when I would see or hear from Mike. What would be my reaction? I asked God how to handle it, but God did not say anything. I know the day would come because God was preparing me with such sweet spirit. I was waiting on closure. I could not move forward without having closure.

The dreams and visions of us still together would not stop, so I asked God to deliver me from that bondage.

I knew in my spirit it was going to be soon that I would hear from Mike. He kept coming in my dreams so much. I looked for things to happen one way, and God brought them his way. In December 2017, Mike sent me a message via Messenger on Facebook. I did not respond. On April 5, 2018, Mike tried to contact me again. He sent me another message. I tried to delete the message and accidentally tapped the wrong button. The phone started dialing Mike. I kept tapping on the button until I disconnected the call, but by that time, the call had gone through. So Mike called me back through Messenger. I answered the call. Mike talked to me as if he had not done anything to me. During the call, I started feeling strong. I said to Mike that I had to go to Bible study. Mike called me back on April 7, 2018, and started talking again like nothing had happened. Mike wanted me to be friends with him on Facebook. Mike asked for a friend request. He wanted to send me some of his prophet works. As you know, I did not befriend him. I did not want anything to do with Mike. I didn't know where his wife was. I guess he was doing it to her like he did to me. I wasn't not going to play into his game. I just wanted closure, and God granted me to do so.

Thank God for that message and the call; that was the closure I needed. I had to have closure so I could move on with my life. How many know God is good?

God said, "I will never leave you nor forsake you." I did not know how I would react or how I would handle Mike when I heard from him. I was so calm, and that's what I needed. When you go through a breakup, separation, and divorce, we need closure from that person and from the marriage issues and problems; if not, they will follow you through life. I had to be free before I could move on with my life. If you don't seek closure, you will stay in a bind. No matter what you go through, we need to have closure, finished with the past chapter before we could be free to move on to a new chapter in our lives.

I thank God for freeing me from the past; it can be a heavy load to carry. Ladies and gentlemen, if you don't have closure from your past marriage, what will happen is you will bring the bondage from your previous marriage into the new marriage. The issue and problems you had previously will follow you to the new marriage. You will be bringing them with you. The old evil spirit that was in the old marriage is now in the new marriage. Get closure before moving forward into a new relationship so you can have a healthy life and healthy marriage. I know that Jesus brought me through, and he will do the same for you. *God is no respecter of persons.*

Chapter 33

New Beginning

I thank God that he gave me a new beginning and chance to reach out to meet goals in my life. When I came to Columbus, Ohio, in search for a career opportunity, I asked God to give me an office with my name on my desk one day. When I was doing janitorial work at night, I was cleaning the offices. I stopped and looked at the offices and said that one day I will have my name on my desk. That was a big step for me coming from my experience in the South, the types of low-paying jobs I had. The increase in pay I had here in Ohio was a big step-up for me.

Jesus came into my life on January 20, 1989. He picked me up out of the mud and miry clay, turned me around, and placed my feet on solid ground. I have been blessed, and I thank God for the blessing. When you ask God to do something for you, it might be five years or ten years, and God will come through; just keep asking, seeking, and knocking. Don't stop praying until you get your breakthrough. God will come through for you; he is always present.

When Jesus saved me in 1989, I had been crying out to him to go back to him. I did not know how to go back to Jesus, so I kept seeking and crying out to him, and one January night, he brought me back home to him. I did not know it would take tragedy to bring me back to him. A friend of mine got killed in order to get my attention. My eyes were opened that night at the club when a friend of mine got killed before my eyes. The gunman killed a friend of mine, and the gunman walked over to me and looked at me. I went down on my knees praying to God to save me. I did not want to die like that and be lost throughout eternity. That night when God brought me out of the club, he saved my life. I don't know how I got home, but I had to thank Jesus for driving me home.

When I went to bed that night, I asked the Lord Jesus to come into my life, change me, and make me a new creation in him. When I woke up the next morning, I was a knew creature. Old things were gone. I was a new creation in Jesus Christ. I heard that you could be changed overnight. It was no longer hearsay; it was a reality that had taken place in my life; it was real. The places I used to go I did not go anymore; things I used to do I did not do them anymore. Drinking, I did not do it anymore; the taste was going out of my mouth. I had a bar in my basement. I got rid of the bar, all the alcohol, and I did not go out clubbing anymore. I had not been in a bar since, unless it has a restaurant built into it. Sometimes I might be in a group, and we eat at a restaurant and bar together. I turned the past things over to Jesus who cleaned me up. I am so grateful for Jesus.

I gave it all up for Jesus overnight who saved me from hell. In the Bible, it says you can change overnight; that was me. My family and friends made fun of me. They even set goals saying I would be back out into the world in three months; it did not happen, so they gave me six months; it still did not happen. Then they said it would be in one year.

It did not happen. I have been saved, a believer for thirty-one years, and I am still running with Jesus. My family saw the change. I thank God for saving me. I wanted to be saved. I had to come to reality that there was nothing out there in the world but sin and trouble. God changed my lifestyle and my friends who had stopped coming around me; they did not want to have anything to do with me. I talked with my friends and asked them to come to church with me. Some of them came to church a few times, but they stopped coming. My old friend stopped coming around me, stopped talking to me and calling me as well. My old friends did not want to have any part of the new person in me.

At first I thought my friends had rejected me, but they did not. It was Jesus who lived in me. I am saved and filled with the Holy Spirit. I was no longer my own. I had been blood bought, blood purchased. I had been bought with a price. I belong to God. I am sealed with the blood of Jesus Christ. When Jesus came and got me, he brought me back to him and filled my heart with the Holy Spirit. On January 20, 1989, I was born again. There were some things Jesus took out from my life. I was made over (new) in areas in my life overnight. I was not the same person. My lifestyle had changed, and the way I used to do things had changed. In time, Jesus changed my friends, and the change in me made my old friends reject me.

I witnessed to my old friends. They did not want to hear me, so we all moved on with our lives in different ways, but I did not stop praying for them.

I do not live the same way before I was saved. As God led me, I started changing my home, taking out things that did not belong in my home, such as images that were not pleasing to God. I guess you are wondering what these things were—the bar with booze, idol status, picture images. I wanted my home to be like when you walk in it, you could feel the warmth, love, and the presence of Jesus. That's what I was told by some people who came in my home and my friends.

My son died on the ship when he was out at sea in Iraq. He was the flagman who climbed up on the pole to the top each day to raise the flag. It was so hot out there that the boots on your feet would almost melt off your feet; that's what he said it felt like on that deck. ACS fell off the pole onto the deck one day and died. The ship's doctor and others in the medical team tried to resuscitate him, tried to bring him back to life. They pounded on his chest. They did everything they could to bring him back to life. He was black and blue from the heart compressions. He was left on the table for dead and covered.

I was in bed sleeping. I was woken up by a voice. It was night here in the United States and day there in Iraq. I heard a voice saying to me, "Get down on your knees and pray." I immediately went to the foot of the bed, went down on my knees, and I started praying, saying, "I didn't know what had happened to ACS but, Lord Jesus, save him." I was praying so hard that big balls of sweat were dripping off me, falling down on the bed and floor. I prayed like that for a while, and all of a sudden, I stopped. Everything was quiet. ACS inhaled a big breath and came back to life on the ship, as he said. I thank God for I heard his voice. If I had not heard his voice or known his voice, if I had not been obedient to the voice of God, ACS would not be here today. To God be the glory.

There was a time when my son was on the ship that his leg got gangrene. It got so bad that the doctor was talking about cutting it off. ACS would not tell me, but I knew something was wrong with him, and I started praying to God for whatever was wrong with ACS to please heal him and restore him to good health. Every time something would happen to him, I knew God would either speak or reveal it to me and let me know in the way he chose. I gave my son a big boom box to take with him. That was the technology on the market at that time. Just in case you want to know what it is, it is a cassette player. I made tapes and sent (ACS) songs of praise and worship and prayers to God and scripture readings and preaching of the word of God and altar calls. He said that on Sundays he would take the tape into the mess hall, and he and some of the crew would have church every Sunday. They had gotten real with Jesus Christ.

I had to be in a place with God to hear him when he tells something for me to do or a place he wants me to be and to know when he is speaking to me. I do remember when Jesus first said to me to go on a fast, I said, "A fast? Me? I cannot fast."

Jesus said it again, "I want you to go on a fast for one day." I said that I didn't know how and what to do. So Jesus told me what I needed to do, and then my phone rang. It was my niece calling me. I started relaying to her what Jesus told me to do. I said to my niece that I did not know how to fast, so she started telling me what I needed to do, and I listened. Jesus was telling me himself, and he allowed the phone to ring so that his prophet could tell me how to fast. I was so hungry for the word to listen and to learn. I did everything God asked me to do, hungry and fearful of making mistakes. I made some mistakes along the trimester stage. I thank God for the trials. They brought me to this point to know who I am and whose I am.

When I was growing up, I never heard my father or mother tell me "I love you" or tell each other "I love you." I knew for myself that they loved one another because they stayed together until death, sixty-plus years. It was common for parents not to say "I love you" because that was the way they were raised. All my life I never heard my parents tell me "I love you." It never came from my parents' mouth. I know they love us. My parents had thirteen children, and they kept all of their children. My mother told us there was a couple who wanted to adopt some of her children, but my mother told them, "If I eat bread and water, my children would eat bread and water also." That was a way of saying that not all of her children were staying together as a family. Back then, family stuck together. That was a way of saying that she loved all of us, not in word but in deeds and action. Back in those days, husband and wife did not take of all their clothing to have sex; they took off just their underwear. They had never seen all of each other's body parts as couples do today. We were raised by our parents back in those days to say "Yes, ma'am" and "No, ma'am" to grown-ups, adults and treat our elders with respect and to listen to our elders. There was a thing about respect. Your parents would slap you in the mouth. When they were talking, you never interrupted parents, and you asked no questions. There are so many things our young generations don't know about, and that is respect because they have not been taught. They are missing out on so much great history.

Chapter 34

My Achievement

Later in my thirties in Columbus, Ohio, I received my diploma in Columbus Paraprofessional Institute for secretarial/word processing in March 1986. The following are other certifications I received:

1. Customer training certificate in general business system in July 7, 1989
2. Certified business owner for alterations and repair
3. Graduation certificate of the National School of Church Ushering, National United Church Ushers Association of America, Inc., ushering department in August 16, 1992
4. Certificate of license for evangelist in September 23, 1996
5. Certificate of license for evangelist with Ernest Banks Miracle Revivals, Incorporated, in September 6, 1997. Headquarter was located at 3887 SW 150th Place Ocala, Florida, 32674.
6. Ordained minister in Holy Band of Inspiration Deliverance Temple Incorporated in June 15, 2003

7. Authority to solemnize marriages conferred by secretary of state of Ohio in October 24, 2007
8. Certificate of graduation in evangelist ministerial alliance 1 and 2 in August 29, 2010, from Rhema Christian Center Ministerial Alliance
9. Certification of completion from Rhema Deliverance Resource Center in November 18, 2014
10. Certificate of completion on understanding God course in April 5, 2008
11. Certificate of completion in breaking strongholds in the African American family in April 8, 2013
12. Certificate of completion on prison ministry in November 19, 2008
13. Completed the prophets classes 1, 2, and 3, and personal workers

I am a traveling evangelist to preach the word of God and works in the outreach ministry. It is a joy when you can go out and reach lost people. I am thankful to God for regaining my strength and health back in him. With God, all things are possible to those who believe and have faith in God.

All things are fitting back in place as I follow Jesus Christ because he has been there for me when I did not know what to do next. So I turned and looked at myself and asked God to show me myself. It was not pretty; it was a mess to look at. All the hurt, pain, anger, bitterness, rejection, and issues I had packed up on top of the Holy Spirit, I prayed, fasted, read the word of God. Soon after doing them for a while, the layer of all those negative spirits started falling away. Anytime you deal with hurt, sickness, and pain, you have to be broken, and with the growth process comes also healing and deliverance. I am made free. Then you have to get closure on the issues that had you weighed down before you can move on with life. If you think that you can move on with your life without closure, then you are mistaken and fooling yourself.

The devil will tell you you're okay. Don't believe his lies. He does not want you to have a future; he wants you to stay in the way you are in past— bound up and in bondage, hurting and depending on his lies. Have you ever been at a point where you did not know what to do? I was at a point of brokenness. God came in and put the broken pieces back together. I was at God's mercy. He healed the broken heart. This is the place where God can come in and put all the broken pieces back together. This is when you hear God's voice because you are at a point that if you don't let God rescue you, it is over, and the devil have won the victory. That is called broken beyond repair. Only God can pick up the fragments and put each one of them in the place where he will have them to be. I was one of the broken vessels. There was a time I only could pray. I love you, Jesus. After brokenness, pray, fast, and read the Word and look to God for healing from the brokenness. He is the only one who can restore us.

Chapter 35

Letting Go

Sometimes we as mothers have a hard time letting go of our sons and daughters when they get married. God taught me how to let go and let him be the God in every area in their life. My son rededicated his life back to Jesus Christ, and he is a new creation in Jesus Christ and filled with Holy Spirit. I thought I had lost my son when he got married, but God let me know that I didn't lose my son but gained a daughter. I not only received my son back, but I received a son who loved God and loved his family. I had the honor to do their wedding (vows) ceremony. It was a blessing that God had to work on my son's faith, walked and shaped him into his image, and now my son and daughter have a good friendship, a good relationship, and a good marriage. They celebrated their tenth anniversary in December 2019.

But from the beginning of the creation *God made them male and female. For this cause shall a man leave his father and mother, and cleave to his wife. And they twain shall be one flesh.* So then they are no more twain, but one flesh. What therefore God hath joined together, let not man put asunder. (Mark 10:6–9 AMP, italics mine)

Just love. Stop domestic violence.

Chapter 36

Learning about Abuse and Domestic Violence

Domestic violence can be so diverse when you don't get counseling or have a relationship with Jesus Christ. Abuse can take its toll on a person's mind and can leave your mind messed up for the rest of your life while you think in your mind that you are okay. Domestic violence will have everything in your body hurting, and you cannot see clearly or think clearly of what is going on or what is happening to you.

Before Mike and I got married, we were in purification for seven days, at least I thought we were. I found out later that Mike was having an affair with Pam and was having sex. We were to purify ourselves, but Mike broke the purification agreement that we had vowed to keep. Mike went on as if he was still being purified. We were to be set apart from each other, to be cleansed in the eyes of God as we enter into our marriage vows. Mike was living in deception from the beginning of our relationship. How did I know it was deception? Pam told me that during the seven days Mike was to be purified to get married, he was out with her. Mike was having sex with her. She told me later when Mike and I had broken up. How can Mike have peace with himself, being a man of God, a prophet of God, and do these things to the one you said you love?

>"Vengeance is mine and I will repay thee said the Lord" (Rom. 12:19).

Chapter 37

Abused

Being abused by a family member is worse than being abused by someone you don't know. I was being violated by someone I trusted and loved. I thought they were there for me and to protect me from the evil people in the world, never thinking my family would hurt me. It is the worst type of abuse. When I saw that person all the time in the family, the abuser wanted me to be silent and to keep quiet about it as if it was okay. I was only a child; I didn't know what was going on or what was happening. Meanwhile it was tearing me apart inside, and I grew up thinking why I was not protected from the sexually abusive predator. My parents trusted Tom with us, thinking he would not say or do anything to us to hurt us. I had to go get wood in the woods with Tom, and that was when he would abuse me. He did not want his son to go with us. I hated to go to the woods with Tom or anywhere with him anymore. I was afraid to tell my parents. One night, Tom started coming in our bedroom, trying to feel us in the bed under the covers.

My sister and I told him to get out and not come back. My sister and I told our mother about Tom, and she had our father put a lock on our door from the inside. If our mother had told our father what was going on with Tom, my father would have hurt Tom badly.

Chapter 38

Recognizing Child Abuse and What Parents Need to Know

The first thing parents need to learn is on how to recognize the symptoms or the withdrawal of their child—the changes in their child's body, their walk, and being afraid to be alone in the room when men are around. There are different types of abuse, and being a parent, you need to know the symptoms of abuse; watch their reaction to things around them. When my children were growing up, I used to keep a close watch on them and check their bodies. I would know if or when something was wrong. Their reaction would say it all; that is if you know your children and love them.

You have to know your children. If there are any changes in their behavior at any given time at home or in school, their grades dropping, that is a red flag. Your child will also do things or make up lies why they were not in school that day. As a responsible parent, you will find out where the problem is, and being a caring, loving parent, you will get to the root of the problem.

Children have so much time on their hands with no supervision, and this causes children having babies at an alarming rate; babies are raising babies. Children have all the time they need to get into all kinds of trouble and violent acts if they choose to walk that path.

Parents are to have order and discipline in their home. You must make the discussion, not your child. You must be the head of your household as parents.

> "Training up a child in the way he should go and when he is old he will not depart from it" (Prov. 22:6 NKJV).

Parents need to get involved with their children's school activities and to know what and how their child is doing in the classroom and how their behavior is in classroom. A child must respond by working harder when they know their parents care and show love for them by attending conferences, some of their sports activities and being there to listen, to talk with them because sometimes that's just all your child needs—your attention. Parents can't deny that they get blamed by their children for problems they are having in school and at home. First of all, behavior starts at home and how you train your child to act. If you teach them with manners and with respect, it will follow them wherever they are and everywhere they go. How do I know that? I did it with my children. We can make great men and women out of our children if we train them up in the way they should be.

How much quality time do you spend with your children? Or do you blow them off by saying, "Not now," and each time your child approaches you, you have the same answer, "Not now." When a child keeps getting rejected, over time he or she turns to other things that will get their time and attention such as drugs, sex at an early age and being a young mother, in and out jail or prison. Why? It's because there's no love, no supervision, and no guidance or spirit guiding from the parents to lead them down the path of success. Children are hanging around with the wrong crowd and wrong environment. Be involved with your children. Know what they are doing, what they are looking at on the internet. Parents, love your children. Be there for your children, and it will make a big difference in their life.

The worst thing happening in school is when prayer and discipline were removed out of school and discipline removed out of the home. How much authority do parents have over their children in these areas? And you are wondering why kids act the way they do. Kids will say to their parents, "If you whip me, I am going to call the police." The parent can go to jail for spanking and have a warrant put out for their arrest as if you have committed a crime. God, help us. The word of God says, "Spare the rod, spoil the child." One of my children tried that story with me. I let her know who was the ruler over my home. I let her know who God had placed to be the head of my household. After that day, my child never came to me with any more nonsense. *Train up a child in the way he or she should go, and when they get old, he or she will not depart from it.*

Chapter 39

Domestic Violence

I lived most of my young adult life with domestic violence. I was abused with domestic violence from my boyfriend before I got married. After I got married, I had an abusive husband who abused me physically throughout the marriage. And my second marriage to Mike, he was a mentally abusive husband. Domestic violence against women is at an alarming high rate, and some of the women are afraid to report the abuse. Women are ashamed to let someone know they had been abused. They think about what people might say about them. Domestic violence touches so many women's lives; it's not a private matter. Domestic violence is protected by women being silent, afraid to speak out. As a woman who experienced domestic violence, I can speak and tell women to get help. Being women, you must examine the way we perceive and change our behavior that might contribute to ignorance, excuses on all forms of violence. Say something; get help.

Domestic violence can affect your ability to function properly. It can affect you verbally, emotionally, and it can control your finances, social lives, isolation, and sexual lives. It wants to control you spiritually. I know it can do those things because I experienced some of them myself. When you live in an abusive lifestyle, you are not surprised at what happens in a relationship. I am saying to all who are being abused to get away from it as soon as you possibly can and as far as you can and get help. Once abused by a person, it's not going to stop unless the person or persons get help. Most of the time the abuser is going to say it is you who is the problem. "I don't need help." They are in denial. I lived in hurt and denial most of my adult life because of the abuse I experienced. I was afraid to speak up. And don't say it doesn't affect you. Yes, it does. Domestic violence can have you so broken and confused unless you seek help.

Domestic violence—it is like a dark cloud hanging over you, and you think in your mind that you cannot escape. God is our deliverer. I used to have nightmares about it. God brought me to a point where I could talk about it, and now I am writing about it, letting women know you don't have to stay in that dark place. God is there to make you free. The abuse that hurt me the most, I still see images of it today. When I was a little girl, I was abused by one of my family members who came into the family through marriage. That is why I say, parents, keep a close watch on whom you let watch your children and be around your little girls and boys. They are so vulnerable, especially around men they trust. Things like this happen all the time. Because it happened to me, it can happen to you, and it can happen in your family and will tear a family apart. I know how a family can be torn apart because I have seen it happen in mine. Sometimes the family does not come back together. There are some family members who cannot get past the hurt. I am praying for my family to be united back together on the natural level, spiritual realm, and walk in the spirit with one another.

Chapter 40

Prayer

God, I pray in your name that your divine protection will be around all women that have suffered some typed of domestic-violence abuse in their life. I pray, God, that you will strengthen, protect, and watch over every woman who has suffered abuse and give them the mind to know that you are there and they need to be protected and to know you are there to guard their heart and want to give them their mind back. I pray for salvation to come to every household and that the Holy Spirit will be their guide. I pray now that every woman that is afraid to come forth to be empowered with your strength to take a stand and take charge of their lives and be healed from every hurt, depression, stress, and all types of sickness that has been caused by abuse. I pray that every organ that is out of place to line up and go back to the place where you originally and designed it to be. God, heal and restore the trusting relationship from childhood abuse that have caused children not to trust family and friends due to the devastation that was caused by said people. I pray, Jesus, that you will have your way with each and every one who has suffered domestic-violence abuse in their lifetime. I pray it to stop, to have your way today, Jesus, in your name. God, I pray for every woman, girl, or boy that has been abused and abducted in the black- market slavery and in sex trafficking who were sold and abused to be free from their attacker and come home to their loved ones. Bring them home and heal their wounds. Heal their body, and heal them, Lord, everywhere they are hurting and fearful because, God, you have not given us the spirit of fear; you have given us the power of love and of a sound mind. To God be the glory. Amen.

Chapter 41

In with the New and Let Go of What's Behind

I finished writing my book last December 2019. While finishing the last details in the book, I just came from a fast last February 1, 2020, at midnight for twenty-one days. While waiting, I was not feeling myself in the natural realm, but my spirit is great. The time spent with my family, friends, and the one who said they love me and who would be there for me last year 2019 were not there when I needed them. I was praying this morning, February 5, 2020, and God started speaking to me. He said that something was not right with me in the natural realm. I started listening to God even though I had repented, confessed, and forgiven for things my family and friends had done to me, and I still walk in love with them and still was hurting. God spoke that there was something that had not been resolved in my life, meaning all the hurt from ex-husbands and family in the past fifteen years and the hurt in 2019. There had been family coming against me on every side, and I had been taking it and had forgiven them. Sometimes family does not apologize for what they have done, and they do not ask you to forgive them; they just go on as if nothing has happened. I went on knowing that the hurt my family and ex-husbands had caused me inside were still there, knowing in time that God will heal the wound. God is doing so in me. I thank him for the healing that is taking place in me.

Family and friends know when they are hurting you, and they know what weapon or who to use to hurt you and know the devastation and the damage it will cause you. Even though I had forgiven everyone, sometimes family and friends get a joy out of seeing me suffer. Some of my family were angry at me, and I didn't know why they were angry, and they didn't know why they were angry; they just based on what they heard. I had created in me a hurt that was causing me to slip into depression last year in 2019 and really did not know what was happening to me, but as I looked back on last year, I was at the point where I ate all the time. Finances were in a bad place. Family was hurting, and I could not go to sleep until the wee hours in morning. I carried the hurt and disappointment around in me for fifteen years, and 2019 was a big factor to it; it was a bad year with some of my family. I thank God for one family member who calls me mostly every day, and you don't know how much it helped me to get through to talk to them, and they did not know how much I was hurting and going through. God let me know on February 5, 2020, after the fast that it was over. I am free from all the past hurt. I am forgiven. I am a new creation in him. Old things are gone, and he has brought on the new—new beginning, new day, and I will have a new season coming my way. God lets me know he is carrying the load for me. The year 2020 will be a great year for me. Rest in him.

Notes

www.ingramcontent.com/pod-product-compliance
Lightning Source LLC
LaVergne TN
LVHW092055060526
838201LV00047B/1398